Heat & Energy

Teacher Supplement

1:1

Answers
IN GENESIS™

GOD'S
DESIGN®

4th Edition
Debbie & Richard Lawrence

God's Design® for Physical World
Heat & Energy Teacher Supplement

Printed January 2016

Fourth edition. Copyright © 2008, 2016 by Debbie & Richard Lawrence

ISBN: 978-1-62691-460-5

Published by Answers in Genesis, 2800 Bullittsburg Church Rd., Petersburg KY 41080

Book designer: Diane King
Editors: Gary Vaterlaus

The publisher and authors have made every reasonable effort to ensure that the activities recommended in this book are safe when performed as instructed but assume no responsibility for any damage caused or sustained while conducting the experiments and activities. It is the parents', guardians', and/or teachers' responsibility to supervise all recommended activities.

Printed in China.

AnswersInGenesis.org   •   GodsDesign.com

Teacher Introduction **5**

Answer Key **15**

   Forms of Energy 15

   Thermal Energy. 20

   Electricity 25

   Magnetism 30

   Waves & Sound 34

   Light 39

Resource Guide. **46**

Master Supply List. **47**

Works Cited **48**

Welcome to GOD'S DESIGN®

PHYSICAL WORLD

God's Design for the Physical World is a series that has been designed for use in teaching physical science to elementary and middle school students. It is divided into three books: *Heat and Energy, Machines and Motion,* and *Inventions and Technology.* Each book has 35 lessons including a final project that ties all of the lessons together.

In addition to the lessons, special features in each book include biographical information on interesting people as well as fun facts to make the subject more fun.

Although this is a complete curriculum, the information included here is just a beginning, so please feel free to add to each lesson as you see fit. A resource guide is included in the appendices to help you find additional information and resources. A list of supplies needed is included at the beginning of each lesson, while a master list of all supplies needed for the entire series can be found in the appendices.

Answer keys for all review questions, worksheets, quizzes, and the final exam are included here. Reproducible student worksheets and tests may be found in the digital download that comes with the purchase of the curriculum. You may download these files from GodsDesign.com/PhysicalWorld.

If you prefer the files on a CD-ROM, you can order that from Answers in Genesis at an additional cost by calling 800-778-3390.

If you wish to get through all three books of the *Physical World* series in one year, you should plan on covering approximately three lessons per week. The time required for each lesson varies depending on how much additional information you want to include, but you can plan on about 45 minutes per lesson.

If you wish to cover the material in more depth, you may add additional information and take a longer period of time to cover all the material or you could choose to do only one or two of the books in the series as a unit study.

Why Teach Physical Science?

Maybe you hate science or you just hate teaching it. Maybe you love science but don't quite know how to teach it to your children. Maybe science just doesn't seem as important as some of those other subjects you need to teach. Maybe you need a little motivation. If any of these descriptions fits you, then please consider the following.

It is not uncommon to question the need to teach your kids hands-on science in elementary school. We could argue that the knowledge gained in science will be needed later in life in order for your children to be more productive and well-rounded adults. We could argue that teaching your children science also teaches them logical and inductive thinking and reasoning skills, which are tools they will need to be more successful. We could argue that science is a necessity in this technological world in which we live. While all of these arguments are true, not one of them is the real reason that we should teach our children science. The most important reason to teach science in elementary school is to give your children an understanding that God is our Creator, and the Bible can be trusted. Teaching science from a creation perspective is one of the best ways to reinforce your children's faith in God and to help them counter the evolutionary propaganda they face every day.

God is the Master Creator of everything. His handiwork is all around us. Our Great Creator put in place all of the laws of physics, biology, and chemistry. These laws were put here for us to see His wisdom and power. In science, we see the hand of God at work more than in any other subject. Romans 1:20 says, "For since the creation of the world His invisible attributes are clearly seen, being understood by the things that are made, even His eternal power and Godhead, so that they [men] are without excuse." We need to help our children see God as Creator of the world around them so they will be able to recognize God and follow Him.

The study of physical science helps us to understand and appreciate the amazing way everything God created works together. The study of energy helps us understand that God set up the universe with enough energy to sustain life and that He created the sun to replenish the energy used up each day. The study of friction and movement helps us appreciate the laws of motion and helps us understand how simple machines can be used to do big things. And finally, studying inventions and technology will not only help us understand the technological world in which we live, but will help us realize that God created man to be creative just like Him.

It's fun to teach physics. It's interesting too. Energy and motion are all around us. We use technology and inventions every day. Finally, teaching physics is easy. You won't have to try to find strange materials for experiments or do dangerous things to learn about physics. Physics is as close as your child's toy box or the telephone—it's the rainbow in the sky and it's the light bulb in the lamp. So enjoy your study of the physical world.

How Do I Teach Science?

In order to teach any subject you need to understand how people learn. People learn in different ways. Most people, and children in particular, have a dominant or preferred learning style in which they absorb and retain information more easily.

If a student's dominant style is:

Auditory He needs not only to hear the information but he needs to hear himself say it. This child needs oral presentation as well as oral drill and repetition.
Visual She needs things she can see. This child responds well to flashcards, pictures, charts, models, etc.
Kinesthetic He needs active participation. This child remembers best through games, hands-on activities, experiments, and field trips.

Also, some people are more relational while others are more analytical. The relational student needs to know why this subject is important, and how it will affect him personally. The analytical student, however, wants just the facts.

If you are trying to teach more than one student, you will probably have to deal with more than one learning style. Therefore, you need to present your lessons in several different ways so that each student can grasp and retain the information.

Grades 3–8

The first part of each lesson should be completed by all upper elementary and junior high students. This is the main part of the lesson containing a reading section, a hands-on activity that reinforces the ideas in the reading section (blue box), and a review section that provides review questions and application questions.

Grades 6–8

In addition, for middle school/junior high age students, we provide a "Challenge" section that contains more challenging material as well as additional activities and projects for older students (green box).

We have included periodic biographies to help your students appreciate the great men and women who have gone before us in the field of science.

We suggest a threefold approach to each lesson:

Introduce the topic

We give a brief description of the facts. Frequently you will want to add more information than the essentials given in this book. In addition to reading this section aloud (or having older children read it on their own), you may wish to do one or more of the following:

- Read a related book with your students.
- Write things down to help your visual learners.
- Give some history of the subject. We provide some historical sketches to help you, but you may want to add more.
- Ask questions to get your students thinking about the subject.

Make observations and do experiments

- Hands-on projects are suggested for each lesson. This part of each lesson may require help from the teacher.
- Have your students perform the activity by themselves whenever possible.

Review

- The "What did we learn?" section has review questions.
- The "Taking it further" section encourages students to
  - Draw conclusions
  - Make applications of what was learned
  - Add extended information to what was covered in the lesson
- The "FUN FACT" section adds fun or interesting information.

By teaching all three parts of the lesson, you will be presenting the material in a way that children with any learning style can both relate to and remember.

Also, this approach relates directly to the scientific method and will help your students think more scientifically. The *scientific method* is just a way to examine a subject logically and learn from it. Briefly, the steps of the scientific method are:

1. Learn about a topic.
2. Ask a question.
3. Make a hypothesis (a good guess).
4. Design an experiment to test your hypothesis.
5. Observe the experiment and collect data.
6. Draw conclusions. (Does the data support your hypothesis?)

Note: It's okay to have a "wrong hypothesis." That's how we learn. Be sure to help your students understand why they sometimes get a different result than expected.

Our lessons will help your students begin to approach problems in a logical, scientific way.

How Do I Teach Creation vs. Evolution?

We are constantly bombarded by evolutionary ideas about the earth in books, movies, museums, and even commercials. These raise many questions: Do physical processes support evolutionary theories? Do physical laws support an old earth? Do changes in the magnetic field support an old earth? The Bible answers these questions, and this book accepts the historical accuracy of the Bible as written. We believe this is the only way we can teach our children to trust that everything God says is true.

There are five common views of the origins of life and the age of the earth:

Historical biblical account	Progressive creation	Gap theory	Theistic evolution	Naturalistic evolution
Each day of creation in Genesis is a normal day of about 24 hours in length, in which God created everything that exists. The earth is only thousands of years old, as determined by the genealogies in the Bible.	The idea that God created various creatures to replace other creatures that died out over millions of years. Each of the days in Genesis represents a long period of time (day-age view) and the earth is billions of years old.	The idea that there was a long, long time between what happened in Genesis 1:1 and what happened in Genesis 1:2. During this time, the "fossil record" was supposed to have formed, and millions of years of earth history supposedly passed.	The idea that God used the process of evolution over millions of years (involving struggle and death) to bring about what we see today.	The view that there is no God and evolution of all life forms happened by purely naturalistic processes over billions of years.

Any theory that tries to combine the evolutionary time frame with creation presupposes that death entered the world before Adam sinned, which contradicts what God has said in His Word. The view that the earth (and its "fossil record") is hundreds of millions of years old damages the gospel message. God's completed creation was "very good" at the end of the sixth day (Genesis 1:31). Death entered this perfect paradise *after* Adam disobeyed God's command. It was the punishment for Adam's sin (Genesis 2:16–17; 3:19; Romans 5:12–19). Thorns appeared when God cursed the ground because of Adam's sin (Genesis 3:18).

The first animal death occurred when God killed at least one animal, shedding its blood, to make clothes for Adam and Eve (Genesis 3:21). If the earth's "fossil record" (filled with death, disease, and thorns) formed over millions of years before Adam appeared (and before he sinned), then death no longer would be the penalty for sin. Death, the "last enemy" (1 Cor-inthians 15:26), diseases (such as cancer), and thorns would instead be part of the original creation that God labeled "very good." No, it is clear that the "fossil record" formed sometime *after* Adam sinned—not many millions of years before. Most fossils were formed as a result of the worldwide Genesis Flood.

When viewed from a biblical perspective, the scientific evidence clearly supports a recent creation by God, and not naturalistic evolution and millions of years. The volume of evidence supporting the biblical creation account is substantial and cannot be adequately covered in this book. If you would like more information on this topic, please see the resource guide in the appendices To help get you started, just a few examples of evidence supporting biblical creation are given below:

The Truth: Much of what scientists observe directly contradicts the ideas of evolution. Certain physical properties have been observed and tested to the point that they have been declared to be physical laws. The first law of thermodynamics states that matter and energy cannot be created or destroyed; they can only change form. There is no mechanism in nature for creating either energy or matter. Therefore, evolutionists cannot explain how all of the matter and energy in the universe came to be. This is a topic most evolutionists tend to ignore. The Bible tells us that God created it all and set it in motion.

The second law of thermodynamics states that all systems move toward a state of maximum entropy. This means that everything moves toward total disorganization and equilibrium. Heat moves from an area of higher temperature to an area of lower temperature, and organized systems become disorganized. For example, an organized system of cells that makes up a living creature quickly becomes disorganized when that creature dies. A house left to itself will eventually crumble into dust. Everything around us says that without intervention, chaos and disorganization result. Evolutionists, however, believe that by accident, simple molecules and simple organisms combined to form more complex molecules and organisms. This flies in the face of the second law of thermodynamics and everything that is observed to happen naturally. The changes required for the formation of the universe, the planet earth and life, all from disorder, run counter to the physical laws we see at work today. There is no known mechanism to harness the raw energy of the universe and generate the specified complexity we see all around us.[1]

A third physical property that contradicts evolution is the small amount of helium in the atmosphere. Helium is naturally generated by the radioactive decay of elements in the earth's crust. Because helium is so light, it quickly moves up through the rocks and into the atmosphere. Helium is entering the atmosphere at about 13 million atoms per square inch per second (67 grams/second). Some helium atoms are also escaping the atmosphere into space, but the amount of helium escaping into space is only about 1/40th the amount entering the atmosphere. So, the overall amount of helium in the atmosphere is continually increasing. If you assume that helium cannot enter the atmosphere any other way, which is a reasonable assumption, then the amount of helium in the atmosphere indicates that the earth could be no more than two million years old, which is much less than the billions of years needed for evolution. This is a maximum age—the actual age could be much less since this calculation assumes that the original atmosphere had no helium whatsoever. Also, helium could have been released at a much greater rate during the time after the Genesis Flood. Therefore, the amount of helium in the atmosphere indicates a much younger earth than evolutionists claim.[2]

[1] John D. Morris, *The Young Earth* (Colorado Springs: Creation Life Publishers, 1994), p. 43. See also www.answersingenesis.org/go/thermodynamics.

[2] Ibid., pp. 83–85.

Evolutionary Myth: Changes in the earth's magnetic field indicate an earth that is billions of years old.

The Truth: Most scientists agree on some fundamental facts concerning the earth's magnetic field. The earth is a giant electromagnet. The earth is surrounded by a magnetic field that is believed to be generated by current flowing through the interior of the earth. And there is evidence that the magnetic field of the earth has reversed several times. Also, nearly everyone agrees that the magnetic field is decreasing. The disagreement between evolutionists and creationists concerns how long it takes for the earth's magnetic field to change and what caused or causes the changes. Evolutionists believe that the magnetic field slowly decreases over time, reverses, and then slowly increases again. There are some serious problems with this idea. First, when the magnetic field is very low the earth would have no protection from very harmful radiation from the sun. This would be detrimental to life on earth. Second, at the current rate of decay, the magnetic field of the earth would lose half its energy about every 1,460 years. If the rate of decay is constant, the magnetic field would have been so strong only 20,000 years ago that it would have caused massive heating in the earth's crust and would have killed all life on earth. This supports the idea of an earth that is only about 6,000 years old, as taught in the Bible.

Creationists believe that the magnetic field reversals happened very quickly, and that the decay rate is fairly constant. One study of a lava flow indicated that reversals occurred in only 15 days. Thus, the reversals likely happened as a result of the Genesis Flood when the tectonic plates were moving and the earth's crust was in upheaval.[3]

[3] Ibid., pp. 74–83.

Despite the claims of many scientists, if you examine the evidence objectively, it is obvious that evolution and millions of years have not been proven. You can be confident that if you teach that what the Bible says is true, you won't go wrong. Instill in your student a confidence in the truth of the Bible in all areas. If scientific thought seems to contradict the Bible, realize that scientists often make mistakes, but God does not lie. At one time scientists believed that the earth was the center of the universe, that living things could spring from non-living things, and that blood-letting was good for the body. All of these were believed to be scientific facts but have since been disproved, but the Word of God remains true. If we use modern "science" to interpret the Bible, what will happen to our faith in God's Word when scientists change their theories yet again?

Integrating the Seven C's

The Seven C's is a framework in which all of history, and the future to come, can be placed. As we go through our daily routines we may not understand how the details of life connect with the truth that we find in the Bible. This is also the case for students. When discussing the importance of the Bible you may find yourself telling students that the Bible is relevant in everyday activities. But how do we help the younger generation see that? The Seven C's are intended to help.

The Seven C's can be used to develop a biblical worldview in students, young or old. Much more than entertaining stories and religious teachings, the Bible has real connections to our everyday life. It may be hard, at first, to see how many connections there are, but with practice, the daily relevance of God's Word will come alive. Let's look at the Seven C's of History and how each can be connected to what the students are learning.

Creation

God perfectly created the heavens, the earth, and all that is in them in six normal-length days around 6,000 years ago.

This teaching is foundational to a biblical worldview and can be put into the context of any subject. In science, the amazing design that we see in nature—whether in the veins of a leaf or the complexity of your hand—is all the handiwork of God. Virtually all of the lessons in *God's Design for Science* can be related to God's creation of the heavens and earth.

Other contexts include:

Natural laws—any discussion of a law of nature naturally leads to God's creative power.

DNA and information—the information in every living thing was created by God's supreme intelligence.

Mathematics—the laws of mathematics reflect the order of the Creator.

Biological diversity—the distinct kinds of animals that we see were created during the Creation Week, not as products of evolution.

Art—the creativity of man is demonstrated through various art forms.

History—all time scales can be compared to the biblical time scale extending back about 6,000 years.

Ecology—God has called mankind to act as stewards over His creation.

Corruption

After God completed His perfect creation, Adam disobeyed God by eating the forbidden fruit. As a result, sin and death entered the world, and the world has been in decay since that time. This point is evident throughout the world that we live in. The struggle for survival in animals, the death of loved ones, and the violence all around us are all examples of the corrupting influence of sin.

Other contexts include:

Genetics—the mutations that lead to diseases, cancer, and variation within populations are the result of corruption.

Biological relationships—predators and parasites result from corruption.

History—wars and struggles between mankind, exemplified in the account of Cain and Abel, are a result of sin.

Catastrophe

God was grieved by the wickedness of mankind and judged this wickedness with a global Flood. The Flood covered the entire surface of the earth and killed all air-breathing creatures that were not aboard the Ark. The eight people and the animals aboard the Ark replenished the earth after God delivered them from the catastrophe.

The catastrophe described in the Bible would naturally leave behind much evidence. The studies of geology and of the biological diversity of animals on the planet are two of the most obvious applications of this event. Much of scientific understanding is based on how a scientist views the events of the Genesis Flood.

Other contexts include:

Biological diversity—all of the birds, mammals, and other air-breathing animals have populated the earth from the original kinds which left the Ark.

Geology—the layers of sedimentary rock seen in road-cuts, canyons, and other geologic features are testaments to the global Flood.

Geography—features like mountains, valleys, and plains were formed as the floodwaters receded.

Physics—rainbows are a perennial sign of God's faithfulness and His pledge to never flood the entire earth again.

Fossils—Most fossils are a result of the Flood rapidly burying plants and animals.

Plate tectonics—the rapid movement of the earth's plates likely accompanied the Flood.

Global warming/Ice Age—both of these items are likely a result of the activity of the Flood. The warming we are experiencing today has been present since the peak of the Ice Age (with variations over time).

Confusion

God commanded Noah and his descendants to spread across the earth. The refusal to obey this command and the building of the tower at Babel caused God to judge this sin. The common language of the people was confused and they spread across the globe as groups with a common language. All people are truly of "one blood" as descendants of Noah and, originally, Adam.

The confusion of the languages led people to scatter across the globe. As people settled in new areas, the traits they carried with them became concentrated in those populations. Traits like dark skin were beneficial in the tropics while other traits benefited populations in northern climates, and distinct people groups, not races, developed.

Other contexts include:

Genetics—the study of human DNA has shown that there is little difference in the genetic makeup of the so-called "races."

Languages—there are about seventy language groups from which all modern languages have developed.

Archaeology—the presence of common building structures, like pyramids, around the world confirms the biblical account.

Literature—recorded and oral records tell of similar events relating to the Flood and the dispersion at Babel.

Christ

God did not leave mankind without a way to be redeemed from its sinful state. The Law was given to Moses to show how far away man is from God's standard of perfection. Rather than the sacrifices, which only covered sins, people needed a Savior to take away their sin. This was accomplished when Jesus Christ came to earth to live a perfect life and, by that obedience, was able to be the sacrifice to satisfy God's wrath for all who believe.

The deity of Christ and the amazing plan that was set forth before the foundation of the earth is the core of Christian doctrine. The earthly life of Jesus was the fulfillment of many prophecies and confirms the truthfulness of the Bible. His miracles and presence in human form demonstrate that God is both intimately concerned with His creation and able to control it in an absolute way.

Other contexts include:

Psychology—popular secular psychology teaches of the inherent goodness of man, but Christ has lived the only perfect life. Mankind needs a Savior to redeem it from its unrighteousness.

Biology—Christ's virgin birth demonstrates God's sovereignty over nature.

Physics—turning the water into wine and the feeding of the five thousand demonstrate Christ's deity and His sovereignty over nature.

History—time is marked (in the western world) based on the birth of Christ despite current efforts to change the meaning.

Art—much art is based on the life of Christ and many of the masters are known for these depictions, whether on canvas or in music.

Cross

Because God is perfectly just and holy, He must punish sin. The sinless life of Jesus Christ was offered as a substitutionary sacrifice for all of those who will repent and put their faith in the Savior. After His death on the Cross, He defeated death by rising on the third day and is now seated at the right hand of God.

The events surrounding the Crucifiction and Ressurection have a most significant place in the life of Christians. Though there is no way to scientifically prove the Ressurection, there is likewise no way to prove the stories of evolutionary history. These are matters of faith founded in the truth of God's Word and His character. The eyewitness testimony of over 500 people and the written Word of God provide the basis for our belief.

Other contexts include:

Biology—the biological details of the Crucifiction can be studied alongside the anatomy of the human body.

History—the use of Crucifiction as a method of punishment was short-lived in historical terms and not known at the time it was prophesied.

Art—the Crucifixion and Resurrection have inspired many wonderful works of art.

Consummation

God, in His great mercy, has promised that He will restore the earth to its original state—a world without death, suffering, war, and disease. The corruption introduced by Adam's sin will be removed. Those who have repented and put their trust in the completed work of Christ on the Cross will experience life in this new heaven and earth. We will be able to enjoy and worship God forever in a perfect place.

This future event is a little more difficult to connect with academic subjects. However, the hope of a life in God's presence and in the absence of sin can be inserted in discussions of human conflict, disease, suffering, and sin in general.

Other contexts include:

History—in discussions of war or human conflict the coming age offers hope.

Biology—the violent struggle for life seen in the predator-prey relationships will no longer taint the earth.

Medicine—while we struggle to find cures for diseases and alleviate the suffering of those enduring the effects of the Curse, we ultimately place our hope in the healing that will come in the eternal state.

The preceding examples are given to provide ideas for integrating the Seven C's of History into a broad range of curriculum activities. We would recommend that you give your students, and yourself, a better understanding of the Seven C's framework by using AiG's *Answers for Kids* curriculum. The first seven lessons of this curriculum cover the Seven C's and will establish a solid understanding of the true history, and future, of the universe. Full lesson plans, activities, and student resources are provided in the curriculum set.

We also offer bookmarks displaying the Seven C's and a wall chart. These can be used as visual cues for the students to help them recall the information and integrate new learning into its proper place in a biblical worldview.

Even if you use other curricula, you can still incorporate the Seven C's teaching into those. Using this approach will help students make firm connections between biblical events and every aspect of the world around them, and they will begin to develop a truly biblical worldview and not just add pieces of the Bible to what they learn in "the real world."

Forms of Energy

Forms of Energy

It works!

Supply list

Copy of "Energy Conversion" worksheet

Supplies for Challenge

Copy of "Energy Chains" worksheet

Energy Conversion worksheet

Initial energy type	Object	Final energy type
Chemical	Battery	Electrical
Electrical or Chemical (gas)	Stove	**Heat**
Electrical	Mixer	**Mechanical**
Electrical	Radio	**Sound**
Electrical	Light bulb	**Light and Heat**
Sound/Electrical	Telephone	**Electrical/Sound**
Chemical or Electrical	Car engine	**Mechanical**
Mechanical	Piano	**Sound**
Electrical	Motor	**Mechanical**
Chemical or Mechanical	Generator	**Magnetic/Electrical**
Electrical	Curling iron	**Heat**
Electrical	Vacuum cleaner	**Mechanical**
Chemical	Human body	**Heat and Mechanical**
Mechanical	Computer keyboard	**Electrical**

What did we learn?

- What is the scientific definition of energy? **The ability to do work.**
- What are some of the types of energy recognized by scientists? **Mechanical, chemical, nuclear, thermal, electrical, sound, light, gravitational, kinetic, and potential.**
- Which types of energy can be converted into other types of energy? **Pretty much all forms can be converted to other forms, although it is unlikely to convert most forms of energy into nuclear energy.**

Taking it further

- Which types of energy are defined by the energy in the atoms or parts of atoms? **Chemical, nuclear, thermal, and electrical.**
- Which types of energy can travel through space? **Electromagnetic waves, which include light and infrared radiation.**
- If the sound of a solar flare were loud enough, could we hear it on earth? **No, sound cannot travel through outer space.**
- What is the final form of almost all energy? **Most energy becomes either heat or light. Each is a form that cannot be easily reused for other purposes, so it is considered lost.**
- If most energy ends up lost, how do we keep everything working on earth? **The sun is continually providing more energy to earth. But on a universal scale, the amount of usable energy in the universe is decreasing every day. This shows that the universe had a beginning—God created it.**

Challenge: Energy Chains worksheet

Accept pictures or diagrams that illustrate the following:

- Coal-powered power plant: **All energy on earth begins with the sun and with the creation of the earth itself by God. The sun provided light energy for plants, which converted it to chemical energy. The plants were converted into coal, mostly as a result of the Genesis Flood. The coal is burned, converting chemical energy into heat energy. The heat turns water into steam, which turns turbines; thus, the heat is converted into mechanical energy.**

The mechanical energy is used to generate a magnetic field which in turn generates electricity, which goes to houses and other buildings where it is used as light, heat, sound or mechanical energy.

- Bicycle: **The sun provides energy for plants to grow which are then eaten by you. Your body then converts the chemical energy in the food into electrical and mechanical energy in your muscles to push on the pedals and then becomes kinetic energy as the chain drives the wheel. Sound energy and heat are also released as the tires contact the ground.**

2 Mechanical Energy

Making it move

Supply list

Copy of "Windmill Pattern" worksheet

Two pennies   Straight pins

Soda straws

Supplies for Challenge

Marble   Ruler or yard stick

Cardboard or wood

Copy of "Potential Energy" worksheet

Observing Mechanical Energy

- Did the penny have mechanical energy as it was falling? **Yes.**

- Did the penny have mechanical energy before it fell? **Yes, it had gravitational potential energy.**

- How did the penny get the potential energy? **You gave the penny potential energy by picking it up and placing it on the table.**

- What happened when the pennies collided? **The first penny slowed down and the second penny gained speed.**

- Explain where the mechanical energy came from and where it went. **Mechanical energy was transferred from your hand to the first penny. Then some of that energy was transferred to the second penny when it was struck by the first one. Eventually, they both stopped because the energy was transferred into heat (and a little bit of sound) due to friction with the table.**

What did we learn?

- What is mechanical energy? **The energy of moving objects or objects that have the potential to move.**

- What are the two forms of mechanical energy? **Kinetic and potential.**

- What are some forces in nature that possess mechanical energy? **Wind, waves, volcanoes, animals, any object that is higher than the ground level, and anything that is moving.**

Taking it further

- Which has more potential energy, a book on the floor or a book on a table? **The book on the table has the potential to move if the table is removed, so it has more potential energy.**

- List at least three ways that machines designed by humans use mechanical energy to make your life easier. **Power tools, electric can openers, electric pencil sharpeners, cars, planes, trains, etc.**

- When does a roller coaster have the most and the least potential energy? **It has the most gravitational potential energy at the top of the highest hill and the least at the bottom of the lowest dip.**

- Give another example of potential energy being converted into kinetic energy. **A skier skiing downhill, a paratrooper jumping from an airplane, an airplane landing, or pretty much anything moving down with respect to the earth.**

Challenge: Potential Energy worksheet

- From which height did the marble roll the farthest? **It should have been from the highest ramp.**

- Why did it roll farther from a higher ramp? **The higher the marble is when it starts its descent, the more potential energy it has, so the farther it will roll before it stops.**

- What did you notice about the speed of the marble as it reached the bottom of the 3 inch ramp compared to the speed of the marble at the bottom of the 1 inch ramp? **The marble rolled from the higher ramp rolled faster.**

- Explain this difference. **The energy is released faster, so the marble accelerates faster and reaches a higher speed.**

3 Chemical Energy

What did you eat today?

Supply list

Copy of "Chemical Energy Scavenger Hunt"

Supplies for Challenge

Research materials on biofuels

What did we learn?

- What is chemical energy? **Energy that is stored in the bonds of molecules.**

- What two complementary processes were designed by God to change the sun's energy into energy for all living things? **Photosynthesis and digestion/cellular respiration.**

- Name two fossil fuels. **Petroleum/oil, coal, and natural gas are fossil fuels.**

- Other than digestion, what is the most common way to release chemical energy? **Through combustion or burning of fuels.**

Taking it further

- Name two non-fossil fuels used in some automobiles and explain why they are chemical forms of energy. **Combustion is a chemical process, and hydrogen fuel cells burn hydrogen instead of gasoline. Electric cars use batteries that produce electricity by a chemical reaction inside the battery. Biodiesel and ethanol are also used as alternative fuels in some vehicles. These fuels are used in combustion so they are also chemical energy.**

- Why are people looking for alternatives to fossil fuels? **Fossil fuels are considered non-renewable. We may eventually use them up, so alternative sources may be needed.**

- Describe one way that chemical energy is used to produce electrical energy on a large scale? **Many power plants burn coal, oil, or natural gas to produce the steam that turns the turbines to generate electricity. Batteries also produce electricity via a chemical reaction, but not on a large scale.**

4 Nuclear Energy

Using atoms

Supply list

Modeling clay

Supplies for Challenge

Research materials on uses of radiation

What did we learn?

- What is nuclear power? **Energy that is released when the nucleus of an atom is changed.**

- What is nuclear fission? **A nucleus splits apart after being hit by a speeding neutron.**

- What is nuclear fusion? **When a new nucleus is formed by the fusing of two or more smaller nuclei or nuclear particles such as protons and neutrons.**
- Which nuclear process is used in nuclear power plants? **Fission.**

Taking it further

- Why is this process used in nuclear power plants? **Fusion only occurs at very high temperatures and fission is more easily controlled.**

- Why are some submarines built with nuclear power plants instead of diesel engines? **A nuclear power plant is more efficient, quieter, and requires less fuel.**
- How might nuclear waste be safely stored? **Most nuclear waste is stored in underground caves in remote areas. Thick lead containers are used for temporary storage.**

Nuclear Weapons

"The Bomb"

Supply list

Copy of "Forms of Energy Word Search"

Forms of Energy Word Search

```
S C H E M I C A L P W A T D S
P O T E N T I A L K L A N E T
U N Q R P J H B I I T V N F
W V R N U L I U L S R V Z E I
M E C H A N I C A L W S M R S
U R O H X Y W G E P A O A N S
G S A F E C I Y H E B L G U I
K I L F M A N H A T T A N C O
I O M N U T D U R R W R E L N
N N I O H S O U C O F T T E E
E L E C T R I C A L A L I A Q
T M A G R E N O D E E I C R L
I A T S O U N D N U O U H O L
C G S O L F L M A M H C S L D
L F O S S I L F U E L X A W V
```

What did we learn?

- What are the two types of nuclear weapons that have been developed? **Fission and fusion bombs.**
- Why are fusion bombs sometimes called hydrogen bombs? **Energy is released as hydrogen atoms fuse to form helium.**
- Why are fusion bombs sometimes called thermo-nuclear weapons? **The fusion reaction occurs at very high temperatures.**
- How are the high temperatures needed for a fusion reaction achieved in a hydrogen bomb? **A small fission reaction is used to produce the high temperatures.**

Taking it further

- What elements are useful in fission bombs? **Radioactive elements such as plutonium and uranium.**
- Why are nuclear bomb tests conducted underground? **To contain the radiation.**

QUIZ
1

Forms of Energy

Lessons 1–5

Short answer:

1. List six types of energy recognized by scientists. **Any six of the following: Mechanical, Chemical, Nuclear, Thermal, Electrical, Gravitational, Sound, Light.**

2. Give the scientific definition of energy. **Energy is the ability to perform work.**

3. What are the two forms that mechanical energy can take? **Potential, Kinetic.**

4. Where is chemical energy stored? **In molecular bonds.**

5. What type of process releases energy by splitting the nucleus of an atom? **Fission.**

6. Who first described mathematically how matter is converted to energy? **Albert Einstein.**

7. Which releases more energy, chemical or nuclear bonds? **Nuclear.**

8. Name two elements commonly used in nuclear weapons. **Uranium, Plutonium, Hydrogen.**

Describe the type of energy represented by each item below.

9. Gasoline: **Chemical.**

10. Rainbow: **Light.**

11. Running rabbit: **Mechanical and/or chemical.**

12. Plant growing: **Chemical.**

13. Tinkling bell: **Sound (also mechanical).**

14. Flashlight: **Light; also heat or chemical.**

15. Thrown baseball: **Mechanical.**

16. Campfire: **Chemical producing light and heat.**

17. Nuclear bomb: **Nuclear.**

18. Magnet: **Electrical/Magnetic.**

19. Computer: **Electrical; can also accept mechanical for keyboard, light for monitor.**

20. Electric can opener: **Electrical and mechanical.**

Challenge questions

Short answer:

21. Write the first law of thermodynamics. **Matter and energy cannot be created or destroyed, they can only change form.**

22. Give three examples of potential energy. **A coiled spring, any elevated item, a stretched rubber band, etc.**

23. What are three types of radiation? **Alpha, beta, and gamma.**

24. List two types of bioenergy. **Wood, animal waste, blubber, ethanol, and biodiesel from corn or other plant material, landfill gases from decaying plant materials.**

25. List two problems with radiometric dating. **False assumptions including none of the tested element was in the sample when it was made; radioactive elements did not enter or escape other than through radioactive decay; rate of decay is constant. Radioactive dating has given inconsistent results.**

Thermal Energy

6 Thermal Energy

Heating things up

Supply list

Thermometer   Calorie chart

Copy of "Thermal Energy" worksheet

Supplies for Challenge

Copy of "Specific Heat" worksheet

Sauce pan   Vegetable oil

Thermometer

Thermal Energy worksheet

- In which areas were the air molecules moving the fastest? **The area with the highest temperature**.

- In which water sample were the water molecules moving the slowest? **The ice water.**

- What were the Calories used for besides heating your body? **Allowing you to move, grow, and perform all the other needs of your body.**

What did we learn?

- What is thermal energy? **The total energy in an item due to the movement of the item's molecules.**

- What is temperature? **The average energy the molecules contain.**

- What is a calorie? **The amount of energy needed to raise 1 gram of water 1 degree Celsius.**

- How are Calories in food related to thermal energy? **The number of Calories the food contains is the potential energy stored in the food. This represents the amount of thermal energy it can supply. 1 Calorie = 1000 calories.**

Taking it further

- What happens to the speed of an item's molecules as its temperature increases? **The speed increases.**

- What happens to the temperature of an item if its molecules slow down? **The temperature goes down.**

- Which has more thermal energy, a melted Hershey's kiss or a giant snowman? **The snowman has many more molecules so the collective thermal energy could be greater than that of the candy, even if the candy is at a higher temperature.**

Challenge: Specific Heat worksheet

- You added the same amount of heat to the oil as you did to the water. Which substance had a larger increase in temperature? **Oil has a lower specific heat than water does so its temperature increases faster than that of water.**

- Do any of the substances have a higher specific heat than the specific heat of water? **Elements with higher specific heat than water include Hydrogen—3.45, Helium—1.25.**

- What are some advantages of substances with low specific heat? **Low specific heat—quickly changes temperature—good for cooking pans.**

- What are some advantages of substances with high specific heat? **High specific heat is good for absorbing heat. Water in a car's radiator absorbs heat from the engine. Items with high specific heat also act as insulators. Insulation in your house helps to keep heat from moving through the roof.**

- List three ways that water is used to conduct heat either for heating or cooling purposes. **Water is used in nuclear power plants, automobile radiators, radiator heating, sweating, etc.**

7 Conduction
Moving heat

Supply list

Copy of "Conduction" worksheet

Thermometer

Several different kinds of containers (plastic, metal, glass, insulated, etc.)

Supplies for Challenge

Sauce pan   Ice

Copy of "Heat of Fusion and Vaporization" worksheet

Conduction worksheet

1. Would you expect the temperature to change most in a container that is a good conductor of heat or in one that is a poor conductor of heat? **A good conductor.**

2. Why would you expect this? **Because the conductor allows the heat to leave.**

3. In which container did the temperature change the most? **Answers will vary.**

4. In which container did the temperature change the least? **Answers will vary.**

5. Would you change the order of any of your containers to more accurately reflect which ones are most conductive? **Answers will vary.**

6. Where did the heat from the water go? **The heat went into the air.**

7. How did the heat get there? **The molecules of water collided with the air molecules and transferred some of the heat. In metal containers, and to a lesser extent in other containers, the water molecules also transferred heat to the container, which in turn transferred heat to the air through conduction. Convection also plays a role. We will learn about this in the next lesson.**

8. Heat-conducting materials should be used for which items in the kitchen? **Cooking pots should be good conductors.**

9. Heat-insulating materials should be used for which items in the kitchen? **Drinking glasses, lunch bags, hot pads, and oven mitts should be insulators.**

10. Why are drinking cups usually not made of metal? **Metal drinking cups could burn your hands with hot drinks or make your hands cold with cold drinks.**

What did we learn?

- What is conduction? **The transferring of heat energy by the collision of faster molecules with slower molecules.**

- What is thermal equilibrium? **When two substances have transferred energy until they are both at the same temperature—they both have the same average thermal energy.**

- Which materials are good conductors of heat? **Metals are good conductors of heat and silver is the best conductor.**

Taking it further

- Give several examples of thermal insulators and how they are used. **Air spaces, foams, fiberglass, wool and other fabrics, etc. Insulation in the walls and roof of your house, winter clothing, insulated drinking cups, insulation in refrigerators, insulation in ovens, etc.**

- What is the purpose of using insulating materials in various items? **Generally, you want the temperature to remain the same for each item—not to lose or gain heat. Some insulators, such as oven mitts, are used as protection against rapid heat loss or gain.**

Challenge: Heat of Fusion and Vaporization worksheet

- Energy is constantly being added to the water. Why doesn't the temperature go up continuously? **Until all of the ice is melted, some of the energy is being used to ovecome the attractive forces between the molecules, not to reaise the temperature. This is also true at the boiling point when the water is converted to steam. Liquid water in a pot can never be hotter than its boiling point (211 degrees F or 100 degrees F).**

- What is happening to the energy when the temperature is not rising? **The bonds between the molecules are being broken—the ice is melting and the water is boiling; energy is needed to break these bonds.**

8 Convection

Currents

Supply list

Red and blue food coloring   Clear container

Observing Convection

- Where did the blue water go first? **It should sink quickly to the bottom of the container.**

- How is the current generated by the warm water different from the previous experiment? **The warm water should rise or stay close to the top and not sink as quickly as the cold water did.**

What did we learn?

- What is convection? **The movement of heat by currents.**

- What causes convection? **Gravity causes denser materials to sink below lighter materials.**

- How does convection affect the weather on earth? **Heat from the sun causes convection currents in the air, resulting in winds and movement of weather systems.**

Taking it further

- Why does convection allow materials to heat or cool faster? **Convection brings new molecules in contact with each other, allowing conduction to occur at a faster rate.**

- Ideally, where would you place heating vents to most efficiently warm a house? **Ideally, they would be on the floor. Convection would cause the warmer air to rise so the whole room would feel warmer. However, often they are placed on the ceiling, forcing the warmer air down so there is more mixing of the air in the room.**

- Ideally, where would you place air conditioning vents to most efficiently cool a house? **Ideally, they would be on the ceiling. Convection would cause the cool air to fall, so the whole room would feel cooler.**

Challenge: Appliance Design

- **Refrigerator should have cooling coils on top to create needed convection currents. Stove should have heating coils on the bottom to create needed convection currents. Both need insulation around the outside.**

9 Radiation

Don't get sunburned!

Supply list

Copy of "Radiated Energy" worksheet

2 cups   Black paper

White paper   Thermometer

Tape

Supplies for Challenge

Copy of "Understanding a Thermos" worksheet

Thermos (optional)

Testing For Radiated Energy

- How does the temperature of the water in each cup compare? **The water in the "black" cup should be warmer.**

- Did this match your hypothesis? **Answers will vary.**

- Why is the water in the cup covered in black paper warmer than the water in the cup with white paper? **Because darker colors absorb more radiated energy.**

What did we learn?

- What is thermal radiation? **Heat that is transferred by way of electromagnetic waves.**

- Which type of electromagnetic waves most easily transfer heat energy? **Infrared waves.**
- Which colors best absorb radiated heat? **Dark colors—especially black.**

Taking it further

- Why do we know that heat is not transferred from the sun by conduction or convection? **Conduction and convection both require the movement of molecules, and there are essentially no molecules in space.**
- What color are the seats in most cars? Why are they these colors? **Most automobile seats are light colors such as light gray or tan because these colors absorb less radiated heat and keep the car cooler in the summer.**
- Why do many people in hot climates wear dark-colored robes? **This may seem like a foolish thing to do. However studies have shown that a black robe is no hotter than a similar white robe, and may actually be cooler. The Bedouin secret may lie in the convection breeze set up when the warmer air inside a loose dark robe rises faster and escapes upward through the porous material, sucking in air from below. These air currents bring cooler air inside the robe and help to keep the wearer cooler.**

Challenge: Understanding a Thermos worksheet

- **The air trapped between lids and between the plastic shell and glass reduces conduction and convection. The shiny surface inside the Thermos helps reduce heat loss due to radiation by reflecting the heat back inside the Thermos. The vacuum between the inner and outer glass prevents conduction and convection from occurring. Tight seal of lids keeps particles from moving.**

Solar and Geothermal Energy

Natural heat

Supply list

Several rocks
Baking dish
Colander/strainer

Large bowl or pot
Thermometer

Supplies for Challenge

Box

Aluminum foil

What did we learn?

- What is solar energy? **Energy from the sun.**
- What is geothermal energy? **Heat energy from beneath the surface of the earth.**
- How is solar energy used? **The radiation is used to heat water in solar panels for use in the home. Also, solar energy can be used to generate electricity.**
- How is geothermal energy used? **The heat from the earth is used to generate steam to warm homes.**

Taking it further

- Why is it difficult to build geothermal power plants in most areas? **The heat from the earth is too far below the surface to be reached economically.**
- Why are geothermal and solar energy being investigated? **They are considered renewable resources and could help replace fossil fuels that may eventually be used up.**
- Why is heat necessary for most electricity? **Heat is used to generate steam for moving the turbines in most power plants. Most electricity is generated in power plants, although some electricity is generated by chemical reactions in batteries.**

Challenge: Solar Oven

- **Oven should have black interior to absorb heat. Shiny surfaces could reflect sunlight into oven. Top should be covered with clear plastic or glass to trap heat. Insulation can help keep heat inside.**

Thermal Energy

Lessons 6–10

Mark each statement as either True or False.

1. _T_ Temperature is the average kinetic energy of an object's particles.

2. _F_ Temperature and thermal energy are the same thing.

3. _F_ Heat moves from an area of lower temperature to an area of higher temperature.

4. _F_ Trapped air is a good conductor of heat.

5. _T_ Thermal insulators are not good conductors of heat.

6. _T_ The sun and gravity contribute to most convection currents on earth.

7. _F_ Convection causes heat to transfer more slowly.

8. _T_ Thermal radiation does not require molecules for the transfer of heat.

9. _T_ Radiated heat travels in the form of electromagnetic waves.

10. _T_ Geothermal energy is generated by the heat inside the earth.

Short answer:

11. Describe the transfer of heat that is occurring inside a glass of iced tea. **Conduction is occurring as heat moves from the tea into the ice. Convection is occurring as warmer tea molecules move up and cooler tea molecules move down inside the cup.**

12. What happens to the molecules of a substance as it heats up? **They gain more kinetic energy and move more quickly.**

13. How would the temperatures of two cups of water compare if they were initially the same and a 1 cubic centimeter piece of steel at 100ºC was dropped into one cup and a 2 cubic centimeter piece of steel at 100ºC was dropped into the other? **The temperature would rise more in the second cup.**

14. Explain the difference between conduction and convection. **Conduction is heat transferred by colliding molecules. Convection is heat transferred by moving currents.**

15. What is the definition of a calorie? **A calorie is the amount of energy needed to raise the temperature of 1 gram of water 1 degree Celsius.**

Challenge questions

16. If you place 100 grams of gold and 100 grams of aluminum in the same oven for two minutes. would you expect the two samples to be the same temperature? Why or why not? **They would probably not be the same temperature after only two minutes. Gold and aluminum have different specific heats so they have different capacities to absorb heat.**

Define each of the following terms.

17. Heat of fusion: **Heat of fusion is the amount of energy required to turn a solid into a liquid.**

18. Heat of vaporization: **Heat of vaporization is the amount of energy required to turn a liquid into a gas.**

19. Melting point: **Melting point is the temperature at which a solid turns into a liquid.**

20. Boiling point: **Boiling point is the temperature at which a liquid turns into a gas.**

Electricity

11 Electricity

Lighting up your world

Supply list

Balloon

Fun with Static Electricity

- Blow up a balloon and tie it shut. Try to stick the balloon to the ceiling or wall. Did it stay? **Probably not.**

- Now rub the balloon against your hair several times. Again, try to stick the balloon to the ceiling or wall. Did it stay? **It should stick to the wall.**

- Why does the balloon stick to the ceiling or wall after rubbing it against your hair? **Rubbing the balloon against your hair removes electrons from the balloon, giving it a positive charge. When it is placed against the ceiling, the balloon is attracted to any excess electrons on that surface and is held in place.**

- How did your hair look after rubbing it with the balloon? **It probably stood out straight and looked very messy.**

- Why did your hair stick out? **The strands of your hair have excess electrons and are negatively charged. Like charges repel, so each strand of hair is repelled by the one next to it, causing your hair to stick out.**

- See how long the balloon will stick to the ceiling or wall. Why does it eventually fall off? **Enough** electrons are eventually transferred to the balloon that the attractive forces are no longer stronger than the force of gravity, so the balloon falls.

What did we learn?

- What is electricity? **The flow of electrons.**
- What is static electricity? **An electrical charge that is built up on an object.**
- What is the law of charges? **Opposite charges attract; like charges repel.**

Taking it further

- Give other examples of static electricity that you have experienced. **Clothes sometimes stick to each other when removed from the dryer. Two pieces of paper may stick to each other due to static electricity. You may have other examples.**

Challenge: Uses for Static Electricity

- Design a way to protect yourself from static electricity shocks. **One possible design is to use an ESD strap. Electrostatic Discharge (ESD) straps are conductive foot straps. One end is placed inside your sock making contact with your skin. The other end is attached to the bottom of your shoe to provide a path for electrons to return to the carpet.**

12 Conducting & Detecting Charge

Keeping your electrons

Supply list

Jar	Aluminum foil	Plastic comb
Paper clip	Modeling clay	Balloon

Supplies for Challenge

Copy of "Integrated Circuits" worksheet

Making an Electroscope

- What happened to the foil? **The leaves of the foil should move away from each other.**

- Why do the ends of the foil move outward? **The charge from the comb is moving down the paper clip to the foil. Because both ends of the foil are now charged with the same electrical charge, they repel each other.**

- You could try this with a balloon instead of a comb. Are the results the same? **Yes.**

- Try generating a charge using other insulating and conducting materials. Which materials produced a detectable charge? **Answers will vary.**

What did we learn?

- What is an electrical conductor? **A material that easily allows electrons to flow.**

- What is an electrical insulator? **A material that does not conduct electricity easily.**

- What is a semiconductor? **A material that conducts electricity under some conditions and does not conduct under other conditions.**

- What materials are good conductors of electricity? **Metals.**

- What materials are good electrical insulators? **Wood, plastic, glass, rubber, cloth, etc.**

Taking it further

- If a material is a good conductor of heat, is it likely to be an electrical conductor or an electrical insulator? **Conductor.**

- Ceramic is an insulator for heat. How well would you expect it to conduct electricity? **It would be a poor conductor. In fact, ceramic is used to make insulators between power lines.**

- Neon is an element in the far right column of the periodic table. Would you expect it to be an electrical conductor or an insulator? **It is an insulator. Conductors are generally found in the left half of the periodic table.**

Challenge: Integrated Circuits worksheet

1. A. **0**   B. **1**   C. **1**   D. **1**
2. E. **0**   F. **0**   G. **0**   H. **1**
3. I. **0**   J. **1**

- What type of gate is shown in problem 1? **"Or" gate.**
- What is its function? **To pass electricity if either input is on/1.**
- What type of gate is shown in problem 2? **"And" gate.**
- What is its function? **To pass electricity if both inputs are on/1.**
- What type of gate is shown in problem 3? **An inverter.**
- What is its function? **To output the opposite of the input.**

13 Lightning

And thunder

Supply list

Wint-O-Green or Pep-O-Mint Life Savers candy
Mirror

What did we learn?

- What is lightning? **A sudden discharge of electricity.**

- What causes lightning? **Friction between rapidly moving air, water drops, ice, and hail strips electrons from these particles, causing clouds to build up a static charge.**

- What is thunder? **The sound generated by rapidly expanding air in a thunderstorm.**

- What causes the air molecules to move quickly enough to generate thunder? **The enormous amount of heat generated by the flow of electrons in a lightning bolt.**

Taking it further

- Why do thunderstorms with lightning occur most often on hot summer days? **The hotter the day, the faster the hot air rises. Faster moving air causes more collisions between particles, setting up the conditions needed for lightning in a thunderstorm.**

14 Current

The flow of electrons

Supply list

Flashlight   Poster board or tagboard
Plastic tape   Coins

Supplies for Challenge

Copper wire   Flashlight bulb
Batteries

Understanding Circuits

- Reassemble your flashlight and try to turn it on. Does it work? **No.**

- Why won't the light come on? **Cardboard is an insulator and current cannot flow through it, so the circuit is not complete.**

- Remove the cardboard and place a metal coin (or a piece of foil) between the batteries. Now reassemble the flashlight and try to turn it on. Does it work? **Yes.**

- Why does it work? **Metal is a conductor, so current can flow through it.**

- Remove the coin. Place plastic tape across one end of one of your batteries. Again, reassemble and try your flashlight. Does it work? **No.**

- Why not? **The plastic is an insulator.**

What did we learn?

- What is current? **A continuous flow of electrons.**

- Name two ways to generate current. **Chemical reaction such as with a battery, with an electromagnet like at a power plant, or with lightning.**

- What is a circuit? **It is a complete path or circle through which current can flow.**

- What is a short circuit? **When current finds a shorter path back to its source without going through the intended device.**

Taking it further

- Why is current more useful than static electricity in many situations? **It allows us to use many electrical devices such as computers, appliances, and power tools.**

- Some flashlights are waterproof. Why is it important to keep water out of a flashlight? **Water often contains impurities which can conduct electricity and can short circuit the current. It will also cause corrosion of the metal and the corroded parts cannot conduct electricity.**

15 Voltage & Power

Making it work

Supply list

Battery   Tape
Copper wire   Flashlight bulb

Supplies for Challenge

Copy of "Calculating Power" worksheet

What did we learn?

- What is voltage? **It is a measure of the electrical potential that can be supplied by a battery or other power source.**

- What direction does current flow in a battery? **It flows from the negative terminal to the positive terminal.**

Taking it further

- Explain how voltage is like a pump for electrons? **The voltage difference between the positive and negative terminals of the battery determines the battery's ability to push electrons from one side to the other. This is similar to the strength of a pump. The bigger the pump, the more water it can move. The bigger the battery, the more current it can move.**

- Explain the difference between power and voltage. **Voltage is the amount of current that a power source,** such as a battery, can push using 1 Joule of energy. Power is how fast that amount of current will flow. Power is equal to the energy per second.

- When might a fuse or a circuit breaker be needed? **If lightning strikes your house, a surge of current could enter your electrical system. The fuses or breakers would protect all of your appliances. Surges in current can occur for other reasons as well. You may plug too many items into one circuit and thus draw too much current.**

Challenge: Calculating Power worksheet

1. How much power would it take to use a printer that operates at 120 volts and uses 4 amps of current? **P=IV, P= 4 amps x 120 volts = 480 watts.**

2. If your flashlight uses two AA batteries, each of which supplies 1.5 volts, how many volts does the flashlight use? **V=3 volts.**

3. If the same flashlight has a 15-watt bulb, how much current passes through the bulb? **If P=IV then I=P/V so I = 15/3 = 5 amps.**

4. Which requires more power, the printer or the flashlight? **The printer.**

5. How much power does a hairdryer use when it is plugged into a 120 volt outlet and uses 15 amps of current? **P=IV, P=15amps x 120 volts = 1,800watts.**

- **Alarm designs will vary, but should include a switch under the door or window that completes a circuit when the switch is stepped on.**

16 Series & Parallel Circuits

Connecting the pieces

Supply list

2 C or D batteries   Copper wire
Tape   2 flashlight bulbs

Supplies for Challenge

Copy of "Voltage/Current" worksheet

Building More Complex Circuits

- What happened to the other light bulb when you removed one in the series circuit? **The circuit was broken so no current could flow and the light went out.**

- What change did you notice in the brightness of the remaining light bulb when you reconnected it? **You should notice that the bulb became brighter.**

- Why did it become brighter? **You lowered the overall resistance of the circuit so more current could flow through the bulb, thus making it brighter.**

- What happened to the remaining bulb when one was removed from the parallel circuit? **The remaining bulb should stay lit and you should not notice a significant difference.**

- Why did the remaining bulb stay lit? **There was still a complete circuit for the bulb.**

- Why didn't it become brighter? **The overall resistance of that path did not change, so the amount of current flowing through the bulb remained the same.**

What did we learn?

- Describe the difference between a series circuit and a parallel circuit. **A series circuit has only one path for the current to flow through. A parallel circuit has multiple paths for the current to flow through.**

Taking it further

- How is electrical resistance similar to the diameter of a pipe for water? **The resistance slows down or restricts the flow of electrons, just as the diameter of a pipe resists or slows down the flow of water.**

- Which type of circuit would be best to use for a string of Christmas lights? Why? **A parallel circuit is best because if one light bulb burns out, the current can still flow through the rest. In a series circuit, the current would stop at a burnt out bulb and none of the lights would light up.**

Challenge: Voltage/Current worksheet

1. Current = **6volts/10 ohms = 0.6 amps**
2. Current = **6 volts/20 ohms = 0.3 amps**
3. Current 1 = **0.6 amps**   Current 2 = **0.6 amps**
4. Current 1 = **0.6 amps**   Current 2 = **0.3 amps**

QUIZ 3

Electricity

Lessons 11–16

Match the term with its definition.

1. _C_ The continuous flow of electrons

2. _E_ A stationary electrical charge

3. _H_ Material that resists the flow of electrons

4. _G_ Material that allows electrons to flow freely

5. _F_ A charged particle

6. _B_ The potential to push electrons

7. _A_ A circuit with multiple paths for electrons

8. _D_ A circuit with only one path for electrons

Short answer:

9. Describe one way to protect the parts of an electrical circuit from a surge of current. **A fuse or a circuit breaker can be used.**

10. Describe how lightning is formed. **Friction between air, water drops, ice and hail creates ionized particles, causing charges to accumulate at the tops and bottoms of the clouds. When the electrical difference is great enough, a bolt of electricity moves from cloud to cloud or cloud to ground.**

11. Describe the difference between a battery and a power station. **Battery—chemical reaction resulting in extra electrons; Power Station—heats water to turn a turbine that turns a coil inside a magnetic field thus generating electricity.**

12. Describe how a light switch works. **A switch completes a circuit allowing current to flow when the light is on, opens or breaks the circuit when the light is off.**

13. Draw a parallel circuit and a series circuit and label each drawing. **See illustrations below.**

Challenge questions

14. In the circuit below, if the battery supplies 6 volts and the resistor is 100 ohms, how much current will flow in the circuit? $I = V/R = 6/100 = 0.06$ **Amps.**

15. In the circuit below, what is the power of the light bulb if the electricity coming into the house is 120 volts and the current is 0.5 amps? **P = IV = 120 X 0.5 = 60 Watts.**

16. What is the voltage of the battery if the current flowing in the circuit is 2 amps? **V = IR = (2) (150 + 50) = 400 Volts.**

17. Describe one use of static electricity today. **Static electricity is used in laser printers to ionize the paper, and it is used to ionize pollutants to more easily remove them from the air.**

18. What would be the output for each of the following gates? **1, 0, 0**

19. Describe the major steps of a lightning bolt strike. **After charges have built up in a cloud the negative charges create a leader, or charged path in the air, toward the ground. As it approaches the ground positive charges create a leader moving up into the air. When the leaders connect a low resistance channel is formed and there is a sudden discharge of electrons. This path is used several times before it dissipates.**

20. What is a transistor? **A transistor is a gate that controls the flow of electricity through a circuit.**

Series circuit

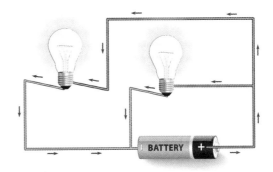

Parallel circuit

Magnetism

17 Magnetic Fields

What's a magnet?

Supply list

One or more magnets | Paper
Iron filings | Bowl
Several straight pins or paper clips

Supplies for Challenge

C or D battery | Iron filings
Copper wire | Paper
Tape

Studying Magnetic Fields

Activity 2:

• How are the pins arranged on the magnet? Are they evenly distributed, or are they concentrated in one or more areas? **The pins will concentrate at the poles of the magnets where the magnetic field is the strongest.**

Activity 4:

• Add a second pin to the end of the first pin. Why does it stick? **The first pin has become a magnet.**

• See how many pins you can add in a chain. Why can't you keep adding pins indefinitely? **The strength of the magnetic field determines how many pins you**

can add. The farther away the pin is from the magnet, the weaker the field will be.

What did we learn?

• What is a magnet? **A material in which the north and south "poles" of the unpaired electrons line up in the same direction and generate a magnetic field.**

• Is the strength of a magnet the same throughout the magnet? **No, the field is strongest near the poles.**

• What is the law of magnetic poles? **Opposite magnetic poles attract and same poles repel.**

Taking it further

• Why does one pin stick to another when the first pin is attached to a magnet, even if they are not attracted to each other away from the magnet? **The magnet causes the atoms in the first pin to line up to form magnetic poles, thus turning it into a temporary magnet.**

Challenge: Observing Magnetic Fields

• What differences did you notice in the magnetic field between the coiled and straight wires? **Magnetic field should be more pronounced and stronger with the coiled wire.**

18 Magnetic Materials

Does it stick?

Supply list

2 or more magnets | Paper | Ruler | Glass
Plastic | Steel BBs | Aluminum foil | Several paper clips
Iron nail | Wood | Penny

Testing for Magnetic Materials

- Which of these items contain iron? **Only the nail and the BBs contain iron, so they should be the only items that are attracted to the magnet.**

What did we learn?

- What materials are magnetic? **Iron, cobalt, nickel, gadolinium, and alloys with these materials.**
- How can a magnet lose its magnetism? **A sharp blow can cause the atoms to become randomly aligned and thus lose the magnetic field.**
- Do all magnetic materials produce the same strength of magnetic field? **No, some magnets are stronger than others.**

Taking it further

- How can you make a magnet? **One way is to rub an iron object against a magnet to encourage the atoms to align themselves with the magnet's magnetic field. Also, heating certain materials and then allowing them to cool can allow atoms to line up with the earth's magnetic field.**
- Test a nickel coin to see if it is magnetic. Why doesn't a nickel stick to a magnet if nickel is a magnetic material? **Nickel coins are not made of the element nickel. They are made from zinc, which is not a magnetic material.**

Challenge: Strength of Magnets

- **Possible tests: 1. How many BBs can be held on the end of each magnet? 2. At what distance will a BB begin to roll toward each magnet?**

19 The Earth's Magnetic Field

Is north really north?

Supply list

Compass
Magnet
Sponge
Bowl

Sewing needle
Ruler or straight edge
Paper

What did we learn?

- How is the earth like a giant magnet? **It has a magnetic field with a north and south pole.**
- How far does the earth's magnetic field extend? **It goes thousands of miles into space.**
- Where is the earth's magnetic north pole? **It is in the Arctic Ocean north of Canada and south of the geographic North Pole.**

Taking it further

- What are some important uses of the earth's magnetic field? **The magnetic field protects the earth from harmful radiation. Also, it is useful for navigation using compasses.**
- What technology has greatly replaced the need for compasses in navigation? **Global Positioning Systems (GPS) have largely replaced the use of compasses. A GPS unit can accurately identify any location on earth within just a few feet.**

Challenge: The Northern Lights

- **Some sources claim that Galileo was the first to use the term *aurora borealis* in 1619; other sources claim that Pierre Gassendi was the first to use the term in 1621.**

20 Electromagnetism

Creating a magnetic field

Supply list

Copy of "Electromagnetism" worksheet

2 D-size batteries

Tape

2 or more different sized iron or steel nails

Copper wire

20–30 paper clips

Supplies for Challenge

Compass

Electromagnetism worksheet

- **You should find that the magnetic field increased when the number of coils increased, when you used a larger nail, and when you increased the voltage of the battery.**

What did we learn?

- What is an electromagnet? **A coil of wire wound around a magnetic material, such as iron, that produces a magnetic field when current flows through the wire.**

- What are some common uses for electromagnets? **Sorting metals, moving magnetic materials, maglev trains, computer disks, video tapes.**

Taking it further

- How can you increase the strength of an electromagnet? **Increase the voltage so more current will flow, add more coils, or use a larger iron core.**

- What problems can occur if you increase the strength of an electromagnet? **The magnet can overheat. Did you notice your electromagnet getting warm?**

Challenge: Polarity

- **Reversing wires should cause the needle to move in the opposite direction. The needle should move back and forth as the magnet moves. This is because the magnet is inducing current to flow, causing a fluctuating magnetic field.**

21 Generators & Motors

Using magnets for work

Supply list

Small appliance such as a hand mixer

Supplies for Challenge

Battery, switches, magnets, etc. depending on design

What did we learn?

- What is an electric generator? **A device that produces electricity.**

- How do most large electric generators work? **They use steam to turn a turbine attached to a wire coil that is suspended in a magnetic field. The moving coil creates a changing magnetic field, which induces a current to flow in a nearby wire.**

- What is an electric motor? **A device that changes electricity into mechanical energy.**

- How does an electric motor work? **A changing current flows through a coil that is suspended in a magnetic field. This creates a changing field that repels the coil and makes it spin, thus producing mechanical energy.**

Taking it further

- List some similarities and some differences between a coal power plant and a nuclear power plant. **They are both similar in that they use steam to turn the turbines in the electric generators. They are different in the ways they heat the water. Coal power plants heat the water by burning coal. Nuclear power plants use the heat generated in a nuclear reaction to heat the water and turn it into steam.**

- List at least two factors that determine how much electricity is generated by an electric generator. **The** speed at which the magnetic field changes, the size of the coils, and the strength of the magnetic field all determine the amount of electricity generated. Also, the efficiency of the power plant in heating the water will determine how much electricity it could generate.

Magnetism

Lessons 17–21

Mark each statement as either True or False.

1. _T_ Opposite magnetic poles attract and similar poles repel.

2. _F_ Most materials are ferromagnetic.

3. _T_ Some magnets produce a stronger magnetic field than others.

4. _T_ Strong magnets can induce iron objects to become magnets.

5. _F_ Current through a coiled wire produces a weaker electromagnetic field than through a straight wire.

6. _T_ A changing magnetic field is required to induce current to flow in a nearby wire.

7. _F_ The earth's magnetic north pole and geographical North Pole are the same.

8. _F_ The earth's magnetic poles never change.

9. _F_ The south pole of a magnet is attracted to the earth's magnetic north pole.

10. _T_ The earth's magnetic field protects us from harmful radiation.

11. _F_ The earth's magnetic field is increasing each year.

12. _T_ Electric motors convert current into mechanical energy.

13. _F_ Generators use magnetic energy to produce mechanical energy.

14. _T_ Magnetic fields are used to store information on computer hard drives.

15. _T_ Electrical and magnetic energy are closely related.

16. _F_ A magnetic field is generated when atoms are randomly arranged.

17. _T_ The magnetic field in a magnet is strongest near the poles.

18. _T_ Cardboard and plastic are nonmagnetic materials.

19. _T_ Nearly all power plants use electromagnetism to produce electricity.

20. _F_ Nuclear power plants only produce nuclear energy.

Challenge questions

Mark each statement as either True or False.

21. _F_ The aurora borealis occurs near the equator.

22. _T_ The color of the aurora depends on the altitude that it occurs in.

23. _T_ You are likely to see more auroras during solar maximum.

24. _F_ The direction of the current through a wire does not affect the magnetic field.

25. _F_ Magnets can be used in only a few applications.

Waves & Sound

22 Waves

Are we at the ocean?

Supply list

Rope

Tracing paper

Radio or CD player

Tape

Supplies for Challenge

Copy of "Wave Characteristics" worksheet

Slinky®

Making Waves

Activity 1:

- What happens to the piece of paper? **The paper moves up and down, but does not travel along the rope.**

Activity 2:

- What happens to the paper? **As the sound waves travel through the paper, it vibrates.**
- How does the movement of the paper change as you increase or decrease the volume? **The more energy in the wave, the more the paper will move.**

What did we learn?

- What is the main difference between mechanical and electromagnetic waves? **Mechanical waves must have a medium to transport them, and electromagnetic waves can move through a vacuum.**
- What is the highest point of a wave called? **The peak or crest.**
- What is the lowest part of the wave called? **The trough.**
- How is the wavelength of a wave defined? **The distance from one peak to the next peak (or trough to trough).**

Taking it further

- Which kinds of waves move faster, sound waves or light waves? **Light waves travel about 1 million times faster than sound waves.**
- What happens to a light wave when it hits a black surface? **It is absorbed.**
- Can sound waves continue forever? If not, why not? **No. Some of the energy is lost to friction and turns into heat so the waves eventually die. Also, some materials absorb sound waves. Finally, if sound waves continued to the edge of the atmosphere they would stop because they must have a medium through which to travel.**

Challenge: Wave Characteristics worksheet

1. If a wave has a frequency of 3 waves per second and a wavelength of 10 meters, what would its velocity be? **V= 3 x 10=30 m/sec.**
2. If a wave is traveling at 10 meters per second and its wavelength is 2 meters, what will its frequency be? **F=10/2 = 5Hz.**
3. If you observe a jump rope being vibrated such that the peaks of the waves are 0.5 meters apart and 4 peaks move in front of you each second, what will the velocity of the wave be as it travels down the rope? **V = 0.5 x 4 = 2 m/sec.**
4. If the velocity of a wave remains the same, how is the wavelength changed if the frequency doubles? **Wavelength is one half.**
5. If the velocity of a wave is unchanged, how is the frequency changed if the wavelength doubles? **Frequency is one half.**

6. Describe how a transverse wave moves with respect to the direction of the vibrations. **Transverse waves travel at 90-degree angle to the direction of vibration.**

7. Describe how a longitudinal wave moves with respect to the direction of the vibrations. **Longitudinal waves travel in same direction as vibrations.**

 # Electromagnetic Spectrum

Different kinds of rays

Supply list

Copy of "Electromagnetic Spectrum" worksheet

What did we learn?

- What characteristic of an electromagnetic wave determines its visible color? **Its frequency or wavelength.**
- Which waves have a higher frequency, radio waves or gamma rays? **Gamma rays have a higher frequency.**
- Which kinds of electromagnetic waves are used for communication? **Primarily radio waves, but some communications use microwaves.**

Taking it further

- Which electromagnetic waves can humans detect? **We can feel the heat of infrared waves and we can see visible light. Other waves can be detected by their effects on our bodies. For example, we get a sunburn when we experience too many ultraviolet waves. Most other electromagnetic waves cannot be detected.**
- Which color of light has the shortest wavelength? **Violet light has the shortest wavelength.**

Challenge: Electromagnetic Spectrum worksheet

a. Radio scanner – **long wave radio or bottom of radio range**
b. Television – **upper end of radio range**
c. Microwave oven – **microwave range**
d. Space heater – **infrared range**
e. Satellite dish – **upper radio to lower microwave range**
f. Light – **visible light**
g. X-ray machine – **X-ray**

- Which item operates at the highest frequency? **X-ray machine.**
- Which item operates the lowest frequency? **Radio scanner.**

 # Sound Waves

Do you hear what I hear?

Supply list

Kitchen timer   Balloon
2 cardboard tubes (paper-towel tubes)

Supplies for Challenge

Stopwatch   Calculator
Copy of "Speed of Sound" worksheet

Hearing the Sounds

Activity 1:

- Can you hear the beeping? **You should be able to.**
- Does the sound seem louder through the tube than it is to your other ear? **It should, because the sound is reflecting off the wall into the tube.**
- How is the beeping different from the sound you heard at the wall? **It should be quieter because some of the sound is absorbed by the couch.**

Activity 2:

- How does the beeping compare to the sound you heard through the air? **It should be louder because sound travels slower through air with more carbon dioxide. This helps to focus the sound more toward your ear.**

What did we learn?

- What is a sound wave? **An energy wave that is detectable by the human ear.**
- How do sound waves move through the air? **By causing the air molecules to compress and expand as the wave passes through.**
- What are some materials through which sound waves can travel? **Air, water, metal, wood, the ground, and many other items.**
- What types of materials absorb sound waves? **Cloth and other porous materials—materials with many holes in them.**

Taking it further

- Can sound be heard in outer space? **No. There are not enough molecules in space to transport sound waves.**
- What could you do to help make a room quieter? **Add more sound absorbing materials.**

- If you blew a horn at the edge of a lake, who would hear the sound first, someone swimming under water in the lake or someone the same distance away on the shore of the lake? **The person underwater would hear the sound first because sound travels faster through water than through air.**
- Echoes occur when sound bounces off of different surfaces. What makes an echo stop? **Some of the energy is absorbed each time the sound reaches a surface, even if most of it is reflected. Also, some of the energy is converted into heat as it moves through air molecules. Eventually enough of the energy is dissipated that we can no longer hear it.**

Challenge: Speed of Sound worksheet

- What difficulties did you experience in making these measurements? **You may have difficulty accurately measuring the speed of sound because it only takes a few tenths of a second for the sound to travel 100 yards.**
- How might you improve your measurements to make them more accurate? **You may improve your measurements by testing sound over a greater distance. Also, performing several trials gives more accurate results.**

25 Characteristics of Sound

Is it high or low?

Supply list

Ruler	Plastic tubing
Funnel	Pencil
Rubber band	

Supplies for Challenge

Bathtub	2 bottles

Experimenting with Pitch

- How does the pitch change? What caused the pitch to change? **The length of the rubber band was changed. As the vibrating part of the rubber band becomes shorter, it vibrates faster and so the pitch is higher.**
- How does the pitch compare to the original pitch? **It should be much higher.**

- Did the pitch change? **The pitch should remain the same, even when you pluck it harder.**
- When did you hear the loudest sound? **You should hear a louder sound when you put more energy into the rubber band by plucking it harder.**

What did we learn?

- What are the three main characteristics that determine the quality of a sound? **Pitch or frequency, loudness or amplitude, and overtones or harmonics.**
- How does the pitch change as the frequency goes up? **The pitch goes up—gets higher.**
- What is an overtone? **It is a secondary wave traveling with the primary wave that has a frequency that is a multiple of the primary frequency.**
- What units are used to measure loudness? **Bels or decibels.**

Taking it further

- Is a shorter string likely to produce a higher or lower pitch than a longer string? **Generally, the shorter a string is the faster it can vibrate, so it will produce a higher pitch.**

- Explain why a trumpet playing a C and a piano playing a C sound different. **The overtones produced by the different instruments are different. So even through the fundamental frequency of the notes is the same, the number and intensity of the overtones change the sound of the note.**

- Why should you keep the volume of your music below 100 decibels? **To prevent permanent hearing damage.**

Challenge: Studying Waves

- What happened to the waves as they reached the straight sides of the tub? **The wave should bounce straight back.**

- How do the waves reflect off of the curved surfaces of the bottle and the tub corners? **The waves will bounce back at an angle.**

- How are the reflections different in the concave curve of the tub compared to the convex curve of the bottle? **The waves should reflect outward from a convex surface like the bottle, and inward from a concave surface like the corner of the tub.**

26 Behavior of Sound

Fun with sound

Supply list

Cardboard tube   String

Guitar or other string instrument (if available)

Glass goblet

Supplies for Challenge

Bathtub

Testing Sound Effects

- Activity 1: Does it stay the same as it goes around your head? **The pitch of the sound will go up as the tube is approaching you and go down as it is going away from you.**

What did we learn?

- What are acoustics? **A building's effects on sound.**

- What is resonance? **When one vibrating material transfers its energy to another material with the same natural frequency.**

- What is the Doppler effect as it relates to sound? **The pitch of an object increases as the source approaches and decreases as it goes away from you.**

Taking it further

- How are sonar and ultrasound technologies similar? **They both use reflected sound waves to create pictures of objects that cannot be seen with the naked eye.**

- Give an example, other than a siren, when you have heard the Doppler effect? **Answers will vary, but a common example is the sound of a racecar or train whistle as it passes by. Also, you experienced this in activity 1 with a tube on a string.**

- Does the driver of an ambulance hear the siren change pitch as he/she drives? **No, because the driver is staying in the same location with respect to the siren.**

- Name some places you have been where it was easy to hear reverberations. **Older buildings were generally not designed with lots of sound-absorbing materials, so they tend to be louder and reflect noises more easily.**

27 Musical Instruments

What do you play?

Supply list

Several glass jars or cups   Straws

Small box   Glue

Spoon   Cardboard or tagboard

Rubber bands

What did we learn?

• What makes music different from noise? **The notes are distinct. They have specific pitches and timing. Music has rhythm.**

• What are the four main types of instruments? How does each make a tone? **Strings—a string is vibrated; percussion—a surface vibrates when struck; wind—air is made to vibrate by blowing; electronic—vibrations are converted into electrical signals that are amplified and turned into sound waves.**

• What is one of the oldest musical instruments? **The harp, the flute, and the trumpet are all mentioned in the Bible as being some of the oldest instruments.**

Taking it further

• How is your voice box, or larynx, like a musical instrument? **It has cords that are similar to strings which vibrate when air passes over them. It is like a combination string and wind instrument.**

• Why is a piano sometimes considered to be a percussion instrument? **It has hammers that hit the strings so the sound is generated by something being struck like a percussion instrument.**

• How can a bugle make different notes if it does not have valves? **The musician changes the pressure exerted by his/her mouth to set up different vibrations to produce different notes.**

• How are string instruments tuned? **By adjusting the tension on the strings, which makes them slightly longer or shorter.**

• How are wind instruments tuned? **By moving the mouthpiece in or out, or covering holes to make the column of air inside the instrument longer or shorter.**

QUIZ 5 Waves & Sound

Lessons 22–27

Choose the best answer for each question.

1. _B_ Which best describes a sound wave?

2. _A_ Which waves have the highest frequency?

3. _C_ Sound waves are least likely to travel through which material?

4. _B_ Which type of wave is quickly transformed into heat?

5. _D_ Which waves can travel through outer space?

6. _A_ Sound waves travel slowest through which of the following materials?

7. _B_ What is the unit of measurement for the loudness of sound?

8. _C_ Which of the following determines pitch?

9. _B_ What phenomenon can cause something to begin vibrating without touching it?

10. _D_ What is the name for a building's effect on sound waves?

Challenge questions

Match the term with its definition.

11. _C_ Increase in amplitude when two waves meet

12. _D_ Decrease in amplitude when two waves meet

13. _A_ Waves bouncing off of a surface

14. _F_ Waves travel in same direction as amplitude

15. _E_ Waves travel at a 90° angle to amplitude

16. _B_ Signal imposed on top of a carrier frequency

17. _H_ Information transmitted as 1s and 0s

18. _G_ Information transmitted as waves

28 Light

It's bright!

Supply list

Boxes or chairs for making a maze
Blindfold
Candle-making supplies (optional)

Supplies for Challenge

Flashlight Book
Desk lamp

What did we learn?

- How is a light wave different from a sound wave? **It is at a higher frequency and can travel through a vacuum. A light wave is an electromagnetic wave, not a mechanical wave.**

- Name three sources of light. **The sun, flames, light bulbs, and fireflies.**

- What color of light has the lowest frequency? The highest frequency? **Red has the lowest frequency and violet has the highest frequency.**

- Explain how incandescent bulbs, fluorescent bulbs, and LEDs produce light. **An incandescent bulb contains a thin wire made of a material that glows when a current passes through it. Fluorescent bulbs contain a gas that emits ultraviolet light when a current is passed through it and are coated with a substance that emits visible light when it is hit with ultraviolet light. LED bulbs contain light emitting diodes which are semiconducting materials that emit light when current is passed through them.**

Taking it further

- Why do people say that life on earth depends on sunlight? **Plants need sunlight for photosynthesis. The sun also heats the earth and drives circulation of air and water.**

- Why do some stars appear brighter than others in the night sky? **Some stars are closer and appear brighter. Other stars appear brighter because they actually emit more light. How bright they appear on earth is a function of both their intensity and their distance from earth.**

29 Color

Red or blue?

Supply list

Paper Hand mirror
Prism (optional) Ruler
Markers Pencil

Supplies for Challenge

Flashlight

Colored filters or colored plastic wrap (red, blue, and green)
Copy of "What Color Will It Be?" worksheet

What did we learn?

- What is the true color of white light? **It contains all colors of visible light.**

- Why does light split when it goes through glass or water? **Different colors of light travel at different speeds through different materials, so the rays of light are bent different amounts as they go through the glass, water, etc.**
- How do our eyes detect light? **Special cells called rods and cones detect light and send signals to the brain.**
- What color of light does a yellow object absorb? **All wavelengths except yellow.**

Taking it further

- Why does light appear to be white instead of all different colors? **All of the colors are hitting your eye at the same time, so your eye cannot distinguish between them.**

- How can we see objects when they do not produce light? **Objects reflect some of the light that hits them. When no light is available, everything looks black.**
- How can we see black objects if they do not reflect any light? **We see them by comparing them to things around them that are not black. Actually, we cannot see objects that are truly black.**

Challenge: What Color Will It Be? worksheet

- **The color shining on the surface may not be pure red, blue or green; the object being viewed may have other colors present besides the dominant color; shiny objects often reflect light of all colors.**

30 Reflection

Bouncing back

Supply list

Flashlight or laser pen	Black paper (not shiny)
White paper	Aluminum foil

Supplies for Challenge

Straight pins or tacks	Modeling clay
Colored markers	Flashlight or laser pen
Protractor	Cardboard
Ruler	Hand mirror

Reflecting Light

- How does the reflection on the wall from the crumpled foil compare to that from the smooth foil? **Less of the light is reflected toward the wall. Because the surface of the foil is no longer smooth, some of the light is reflected in different directions. This is called diffusion.**
- How does the reflection from the white paper compare to the reflection from the smooth foil? **The reflection is probably not as bright.**
- Why? **The paper absorbs some of the light.**
- Again, repeat the test using non-shiny black paper. How does this reflection compare to the others? **Black materials absorb nearly all the light that hits them so there should be very little reflection. If the paper is shiny, however, it will reflect some light.**

What did we learn?

- What is a reflection? **Light that bounces off of a surface.**
- Which types of materials best reflect light? **Smooth, shiny materials.**
- What kind of path does light take? **It moves in waves that travel in straight lines.**

Taking it further

- If light approaches a mirror at a 30-degree angle of incidence, what will the angle of reflection be? **30 degrees.**
- If the back of a mirror is not smooth, what is likely to happen to the image you see? **It will be distorted because the light is not reflecting at the angles you expect to see. It is diffused.**

Challenge: Angle of Incidence

- Why might the angles be slightly different? If your measurements are different by more than a few degrees, what might be the explanation? **Not shining the flashlight at the exact center of the mirror, not marking the lines perfectly straight, error in reading the protractor. Larger errors could be caused because your flashlight beam is too broad.**

31 Mirrors

Mirror, mirror on the wall

Supply list

Spoon   Mirror

Supplies for Challenge

2 small mirrors   Tape
Cardboard

What did we learn?

- What are the three shapes of mirrors? **Plane or flat, concave, and convex.**

- How does a concave mirror affect light rays and the reflected image? **It bends the light inward and inverts the image.**

- How does a convex mirror affect the light rays and the reflected image? **It bends the light outward and stretches the image.**

Taking it Further

- Would you expect the reflected image from a concave mirror to be brighter or darker than the original image? **You would expect it to be brighter because the light is concentrated in one spot.**

- Explain how a periscope uses mirrors. **The light is reflected from one mirror to another to reflect light around a corner or to change its direction.**

32 Refraction

Bending the light

Supply list

Drinking glass   Pencil
Flashlight or laser pen   Milk

Supplies for Challenge

Flashlight or laser pen   Salt
Vegetable oil   Milk
3 clear containers with straight sides

Observing Refraction

- How did the pencil in the water look from the side of the cup? Why? **It appears bent because the light is bent as it passes through the glass and the water.**

- How was the light bent when entering from the top of the cup? **The beam should bend slightly away from what would have been the straight line of the beam.**

- Was it the same or different from before? If it was different, why was it different? **It was bent by the glass, and then bent by the water. The beam should be bent more.**

What did we learn?

- What is refraction? **The bending of light as it changes speed going from one medium to another.**

- Why do items appear to be in a different location underwater than they actually are? **The bent light hits your eyes in a location other than where you expect, making the object appear to be in a slightly different location.**

- What is a mirage? **It is a reflection of the sky above the pavement on a hot day. It occurs because light is bent as it moves from denser cooler air into warmer less dense air near the ground.**

Taking it Further

- Will light bend more or less as it passes through a denser material than through a less dense material? **It will bend more because it slows down more in dense materials.**

- Are you more likely to see a mirage during the summer or the winter? Why? **During the summer, because the summer sun heats the ground more than** the winter sun does, and a difference in air density is necessary for a mirage to occur.

Challenge: Density and Refraction

- Which substance bent the light the most? Which substance bent the light the least? **The salt water should bend the light the most and the oil the least.**

- What are the relative densities of the three liquids? **Salt water is the most dense, water is next, and oil is the least dense.**

- How does the density appear to affect the refraction of the light? **The denser the material, the more the light is bent.**

33 Lenses

Do you need glasses?

Supply list

Small box

Cardboard tube

Magnifying glass

Tape

Tracing paper

Supplies for Challenge

Copy of "Focal Length" worksheet

Various concave and convex lenses

Homemade Camera

- How does the image on the "film" compare to the actual object? **It should be upside down and smaller.**

- Why is the image different from the real thing? **The lens bends the light as it passes through and causes the image to be inverted and smaller.**

What did we learn?

- What is a lens? **A curved piece of glass or plastic that bends light.**

- What effect does a convex lens have on light? **Parallel light rays are bent toward the center of the lens. Images are either upside down and smaller than the actual object, or right side up and larger, depending on the distance from the lens and the lens's focal length.**

- What effect does a concave lens have on light? **Parallel light rays are bent outward from the lens. The image will be right side up and smaller.**

- What is another name for a concave lens? **Diverging lens.**

- Name three inventions that use lenses. **Telescope, microscope, camera, eyeglasses, magnifying glass, and others.**

Taking it further

- Would you expect the image seen through a microscope to be right side up or upside down? What about the image seen through a telescope? **Usually the image is upside down in both devices; however, it depends on the types of lenses used.**

- The image projected onto your retina is upside down, so why don't you see things upside down? **Your brain turns the image right side up.**

Challenge: Focal Length worksheet

- What differences did you notice between the convex and concave lenses? **The convex lens will flip the image, and the image should remain upright in the concave lens.**

- How did the image change as you moved the convex lens closer and farther away? **The image should flip as you move it closer and farther away. The size will also change depending on the distance from the object.**

- How did the image change as you moved the concave lens closer and farther away? **It should change size, but remain upright.**

- How did the focal lengths differ between the various lenses? **The focal length of a convex lens is determined not only by the curvature of the lens, but also by the material the lens is made from. Different types of glass and different types of plastic refract the light different amounts.**

QUIZ 6

Light

Lessons 28–33

Match the term with its definition.

1. _B_ Energy that can be detected by the human eye
2. _F_ Primary source of light on earth
3. _J_ Light bulb that emits ultraviolet light which in turn causes a substance to glow
4. _I_ Light bulb with a glowing filament
5. _A_ Name for range of different colors of light
6. _D_ Device for separating colors of light
7. _C_ Color of visible light with the shortest wavelength
8. _H_ Part of the eye that detects color
9. _E_ Light rays that bounce off of a mirror
10. _T_ Type of image seen in a mirror
11. _M_ Lens that bends light toward the center
12. _N_ Lens that bends light away from the center (**R is also acceptable.**)
13. _O_ Flat mirror
14. _L_ Bending of light
15. _K_ Curved piece of glass or plastic
16. _S_ Reflection of the sky above hot pavement
17. _G_ Part of the eye that detects small changes in light

18. _Q_ The color of objects that don't reflect any light
19. _P_ All colors of light combine to make this color
20. _R_ Alternate name for a concave lens

Challenge questions

Short answer:

21. Explain the difference between transparent, translucent, and opaque materials. **Transparent—light passes through; translucent—some light passes while other light is blocked; opaque—all light is blocked.**

22. What are the two parts of a shadow? **Umbra and penumbra.**

23. Explain why a filter changes the color of light emitted by a flashlight. **A filter only allows light of a certain frequency to pass through, thus the color will be changed.**

24. If the angle of incidence is 27 degrees, what will the angle of reflection be? **27 degrees.**

25. Why will the angle of refraction be different in water than it is in vegetable oil? **Light changes speed as it moves from one material to another. This change in speed is affected by the density of the material it is passing through. Water and oil have different densities so the change in speed will be different.**

34 Using Energy

Converting energy for our use

Final Project supply list

Camera (optional)   Drawing supplies

What did we learn?

*   What are some of the types of energy recognized by scientists? **Mechanical, chemical, nuclear, thermal, electrical, magnetic, gravitational, sound, and light.**
*   What two basic forms can energy be found to take? **Potential and kinetic.**

Taking it further

*   What is your favorite way to use energy? **Answers will vary.**

Heat & Energy

Lessons 1–34

1. Give an example of each of the following types of energy. **Accept any reasonable answers.**

Match the term with its definition.

2. _B_ Heat transfer by currents
3. _C_ Heat transfer by electromagnetic waves
4. _A_ Heat transfer by colliding particles
5. _I_ Material that allows electricity to flow
6. _H_ Material that resists the flow of electricity
7. _K_ Converts electricity into mechanical energy
8. _J_ Converts mechanical energy into electricity
9. _E_ Magnetic fields protecting the earth
10. _F_ Bouncing light waves
11. _G_ Bending light waves
12. _D_ Direction all compasses point

Mark each statement as either True or False.

13. _F_ Electromagnetic waves must travel through a medium.
14. _F_ Gamma waves have the lowest frequency of all electromagnetic waves.
15. _T_ Microwaves can be used for communications as well as for cooking.
16. _T_ Sound waves compress and expand molecules through which they travel.
17. _F_ Metal is most likely to absorb sound waves.
18. _F_ An overtone is a sound that is louder than the original sound.
19. _T_ Sounds over 100 decibels can cause hearing loss.
20. _T_ A building's acoustics determine how sound travels inside it.
21. _T_ Materials with the same natural frequency can transfer energy by resonance.
22. _T_ The pitch of the sound of a moving object changes as it approaches you.

Identify each type of instrument. P = percussion, W = wind, S = string

23. _P_ Drum
24. _S_ Guitar
25. _W_ Saxophone
26. _S_ Viola
27. _S or P_ Piano
28. _W_ Harmonica
29. _P_ Xylophone
30. _S_ Cello
31. _W_ French horn
32. _W_ Panpipes
33. _P_ Cymbals
34. _W_ Flute

35. Draw a wave and label the crest, trough, wavelength, and amplitude.

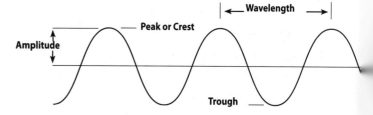

Fill in the blank with the correct term.

36. _Electromagnetic_ waves can travel through a vacuum. (**Light** is also an acceptable answer.)
37. _Mechanical_ waves must travel through a medium. (**Sound** is also an acceptable answer)
38. Electricity causes ultraviolet light to be emitted inside a _fluorescent_ light bulb.
39. Thomas Edison invented the first working _incandescent_ light bulb.
40. _White_ light really contains all colors of light.
41. _Black_-colored objects absorb all colors of light.
42. A lens that curves toward the source of light is called a _convex_ lens.
43. A false reflection of the sky above a hot surface is called a _mirage_.

Short answer:

44. Explain how eyeglasses help correct vision problems. **The lens changes the focal point of the light to compensate for the incorrect focal length of the eye's lens.**

Challenge questions

45. Name three places on earth where convection currents affect the whole world. **Atmosphere, oceans, magma inside the earth.**
46. Explain how the first law of thermodynamics supports creation and not evolution. **Since energy and**

matter cannot be created or destroyed by any natural means, their origin must be supernatural.

47. Name at least one assumption used in radiometric dating that could result in inaccurate results. **The original amounts of radioactive and resultant materials are known; the tested elements did not enter or leave through any means other than the one being tested; the rate of radioactive decay has remained constant.**

48. What will happen to a magnetic field if the current generating the field is reversed? **The polarity of the magnetic field will reverse.**

49. What will happen to the amplitude of the resulting wave if the crests of two waves with the same frequency meet? **They will combine to double the amplitude.**

50. Define the focal length of a lens. **The distance between the lens and the focal point; point at which the object is in focus.**

35 Conclusion

God gave us energy

Supply list

Bible

Resource Guide

Many of the following titles are available from Answers in Genesis (www.AnswersBookstore.com).

Suggested Books

Magnets by Janice Van Cleave—Many fun experiments

Be a Kid Physicist by William R. Wellnitz

Light by Steve Parker—Interesting activities

Sound by Steve Parker—More interesting activities

Usborne Science Encyclopedia by Kirsteen Rogers and others—great reference book for all ages

Science and the Bible Volumes 1–3 by Donald B. DeYoung—scientific demonstrations with Biblical truths

Exploring the World of Physics by John Hudson Tiner—explains physics in clear detail, using ordinary speech

Men of Science, Men of God—100 biographies of Christian scientists past and present

Suggested Videos/DVDs

Newton's Workshop by Moody Institute—Excellent Christian science series; several titles to choose from

Field Trip Ideas

- Visit the Creation Museum in Petersburg, Kentucky.
- Tour a battery store to learn about different types of batteries.
- Tour a power plant.
- Visit a scrap yard that uses giant electromagnets.
- Visit an optometrist's office and learn more about eyeglasses.
- Visit an observatory and learn about their telescope.
- Visit any solar, wind, or hydroelectric energy plants in your area.
- Attend a symphony concert and learn more about the instruments.

Creation Science Resources

Answers Book for Kids Six volumes by Ken Ham with Cindy Malott and others—Answers children's frequently asked questions

The New Answers Books 1–4 by Ken Ham and others—Answers frequently asked questions

The Amazing Story of Creation by Duane T. Gish—Gives scientific evidence for the creation story

Creation Science by Felice Gerwitz and Jill Whitlock—Unit study focusing on creation

Creation: Facts of Life by Gary Parker—Comparison of the evidence for creation and evolution

The Young Earth by John D. Morris—Lots of facts disproving old-earth ideas

Master Supply List

The following table lists all the supplies used for *God's Design for the Physical World: Heat & Energy* activities. You will need to look up the individual lessons in the student book to obtain the specific details for the individual activities (such as quantity, color, etc.). The letter *c* denotes that the lesson number refers to the challenge activity. Common supplies such as colored pencils, construction paper, markers, scissors, tape, etc., are not listed.

Supplies needed (see lessons for details)	Lesson
Aluminum foil	10, 12, 14, 18, 30
Balloons	11, 12, 24
Batteries (2 D cells)	14c, 15, 16, 17, 20, 21c
BBs (steel)	18
Bible	35
Box (small)	10c, 27, 33
Calculator	24c
Camera (optional)	34
Candle-making supplies (optional)	28
Cardboard tubes (paper towel rolls)	24, 26, 33
Coins (pennies, nickels)	2, 14, 18
Colander/strainer	10
Colored filters or colored plastic wrap	29c
Comb (plastic)	12
Compass (navigational)	19, 20c
Flashlights	14, 15, 16, 28, 29, 30, 32
Food coloring	8
Funnel	25
Iron filings	17
Jars	12, 27
Lenses	33c
Life Savers candies	13
Magnets	17, 18, 19, 21
Magnifying glass	33

Supplies needed (see lessons for details)	Lesson
Marbles	2c
Milk	32c
Mirror (hand)	29, 30, 31
Modeling clay	4, 12, 30c
Nails (iron)	18, 20
Needle (sewing)	19
Paint (black)	10c
Paper clips	12, 17, 18, 20
Plastic bottle (2-liter, empty)	25c
Poster board/cardboard/tagboard	2, 14, 19, 27, 30, 31
Prism (optional)	29
Protractor	30c
Radio or CD player	22
Rope	22
Rubber bands	25, 27
Salt	32c
Slinky® (metal)	22c
Sponge	19
Stopwatch	24c
Straight pins	2, 30c
Straws	2, 27
String	26
String instrument (optional)	26
Thermometer	6, 7, 9, 10
Thermos (optional)	9c
Timer (with beep)	24
Tracing paper	22, 33
Tubing (clear plastic)	25
Vegetable oil	6c, 32c
Wire (copper)	14, 15, 16, 17, 20
Wood (block)	2, 18
Yard stick/meter stick and ruler	2, 18, 19, 25, 29, 30

Works Cited

Bellis, Mary. "Inventors: The History Behind the Thermometer." http://inventors.about.com/library/inventors/blthermometer.htm.

Bracchini, Miguel A. "The History and Ethics Behind the Manhattan Project." http://www.me.utexas.edu/~uer/manhattan.

Burnie, David. *Light*. New York: Dorling Kindersley, 1992.

Day, Trevor. *Light*. Austin: Raintree Steck-Vaughn Publishers, 1998.

dePinna, Simon. *Sound*. Austin: Raintree Steck-Vaughn Publishers, 1998.

Drewry, Richard D., Jr. "What Man Devised that He Might See." http://www.teagleoptometry.com/history.htm.

"Earth's Inconstant Magnetic Filed." http://science.nasa.gov/headlines/y2003/29dec_magneticfield.htm.

Fradin, Dennis B. *Nuclear Energy*. Chicago: Children's Press, 1987.

Gerwitz, Felice, and Jill Whitlock. *Creation Science: A Study Guide to Creation!* Ft. Meyers: Media Angels, 1997.

Hammond, Susan. *Mr. Bach Comes to Call*. Pickering, Ontario: The Children's Group, 1998.

"Henry, Joseph." http://etcweb.princeton.edu/CampusWWW/Companion/henry_joseph.html.

"Heritage Faraday Page." http://www.rigb.org/contentControl?pg=4&filter=pd&action=detail&section=1391.

"How Hard Disks Work." http://www.howstuffworks.com/hard-disk.htm.

"J.S. Bach: Education and Career." http://jan.ucc.nau.edu/~tas3/life.html.

Jenkins, John E., and George Mulfinger, Jr. *Basic Science for Christian Schools*. Greenville: Bob Jones University Press, 1983.

Jennings, Terry. *Electricity and Magnetism*. Toronto: Templar Company, 1992.

"Johann Sebastian Bach." http://w3.rz-berlin.mpg.de/cmp/bachjs.html.

"Johann Sebastian Bach." http://www.baroquemusic.org/bqxjsbach.html.

"Joseph Henry." http://chem.ch.huji.ac.il/~eugeniik/history/henry.html.

"Joseph Henry." http://www.aip.org/history/gap/Henry/Henry.html.

Lafferty, Peter. *Energy and Light*. New York: Shooting Star Press, 1993.

Lafferty, Peter. *Light and Sound*. New York: Benchmark Books, 1996.

Lemley, Brad. "Nuclear Planet." http://discovermagazine.com/2002/aug/cover/.

Mulfinger, George, and Donald Snyder. *Earth Science for Christian Schools*. Greenville: Bob Jones University Press, 1995.

"The Manhattan Project." http://www.atomicmuseum.com/tour/manhattanproject.cfm.

"Michael Faraday." http://www-groups.dcs.st-and.ac.uk/~history/Mathematicians/Faraday.html.

Morris, John. *The Young Earth*. Colorado Springs: Master Books, 1993.

Parker, Steve. *Electricity*. London: Dorling Kindersley, 1992.

Parker, Steve. *Light*. Milwaukee: Gareth Stevens Publishing, 1997.

Parker, Steve. *Sound*. Milwaukee: Gareth Stevens Publisher, 1997.

"Regions of the Electromagnetic Spectrum." http://imagine.gsfc.nasa.gov/docs/science/know_l1/spectrum_chart.html.

Richards, Julie. *Future Energy—Geothermal Energy and Boienergy*. North Mankato: Smart Apple Media, 2004.

Rogers, Kirsteen, and others. *Usborne Science Encyclopedia*. London: Usborne Publishing, 2002.

Sarfati, Jonathan, PhD. "Is the Earth's Magnetic Field About to Flip?" http://www.answersingenesis.org/docs2003/0401magnetic_flip.asp.

Sherman, Josepha. *Hydroelectric Power*. Mankato: Capstone Press, 2004.

"Sun Flips Magnetic Field." http://archives.cnn.com/2001/TECH/space/02/16/sun.flips/index.html.

VanCleave, Janice. *Magnets*. New York: John Wiley & Sons, 1993.

Wellnitz, William R., PhD. *Be a Kid Physicist*. Blue Ridge Summit: TAB Books, 1993